TRADING CHART PATTERN & CANDLESTICK

ABHISHEK KUMAR

Made with ♥ on the Notion Press Platform
www.notionpress.com

To mr. market

Thanks for always teaching

Contents

Acknowledgements *vii*

Preface *ix*

1. Bullish Marubozu 1

2. Bearish Marubozu 3

3. Spinning Top 5

Part 1

4. The Dojis 9

5. The Hammer 11

The Hanging Man

The Shooting Star

6. The Engulfing Pattern 17

Bullish Engulfing

Bearish Engulfing

7. The Piercing Pattern 23

8. The Dark Cloud Cover 26

9. The Bullish Harami Pattern 28

10. The Bearish Harami Pattern 30

11. The Morning Star Pattern 33

12. The Evening Star Pattern 35

13. SUPPORT AND RESISTANCE 37

14. Double Bottom 39

15. Double Top 41

16. Head And Shoulder 43

17. Inverse Head And Shoulders 46

Contents

18. Cup And Handle Pattern 48

19. Ascending Triangle 49

20. Symmetrical Triangle 51

21. Rounding Bottom 53

22. Pannants Or Flags 54

Advise 57

ACKNOWLEDGEMENTS

Writing a book isn't something I did alone. I want to thank thank:

My family, for always supporting and encouraging me. Your love and patience meant everything.

My friend, who kept me going t=with thri endless suppory and enocuragement.

My mentor, [mr. market], for guiding me and sharing their wisdom, which kept me inspired.

And to you, the readers, thank you for making it all worthwhile. Your interest and support mean the world to me.

Without all of you, this book wouldn't habe been possible

PREFACE

Hello! I'm thrilled to share this book, [TRADING CHART PATTERN AND CANDLESTICKS], with you

I wrote this book beacause to share a small knowledge with you what I learn for mr. market in several years. It's been quite a journey, with lots of learning along the way.

I want to thank my family, as their support meant everything.

in thease pages,I hope you will find and learn to start their journey in stockmarket.

Thank you for being there. let's learn together!

Abhishek kumar

I

Bullish Marubozu

Enter Caption

A Bullish Marubozu pattern is defined by a long green (or blue) candlestick with no shadows projecting from either end—only body mass all the way. The opening price is equivalent to the low for the time, while the ending price is close to the high.

The Bullish Marubozu is especially powerful when it forms at the end of a downtrend or breaks through a resistance level. In these cases, it acts like a green light for the bulls, signaling that it's their turn to run the show

II

Bearish Marubozu

Enter Caption

A bearish Marubozu pattern is defined by a lengthy red (or black) candlestick with no upper or lower shadows. The period's opening price coincides with the high, while the ending price corresponds to the low.

When you see a Bearish Marubozu, it means that sellers are not only in control, but also driving the market lower with tremendous power. There is little to no buying activity, which frequently indicates that a negative trend is likely to continue.

III

Spinning top

Enter Caption

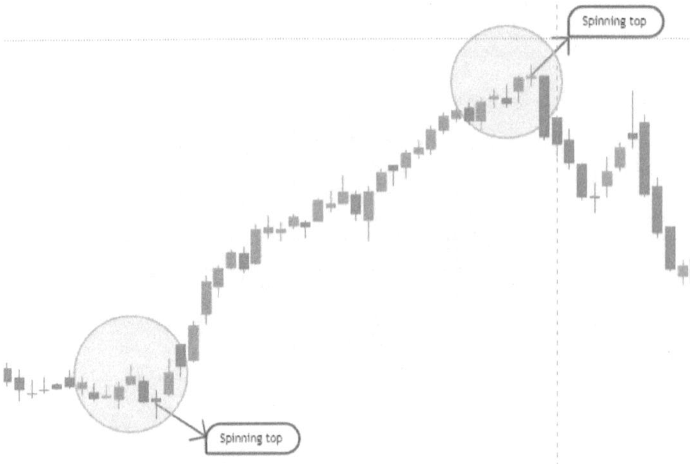

Enter Caption

Spinning tops signal hesitation in the asset, while extended upper and lower shadows suggest no significant price change between the open and close. The bulls moved the price substantially higher, while the bears brought it sharply lower, but the price eventually closed roughly where it opened. This uncertainty may indicate more sideways movement, particularly if the spinning top happens within a predetermined range. It may also indicate a likely price reversal if it comes after a price increase or decrease.

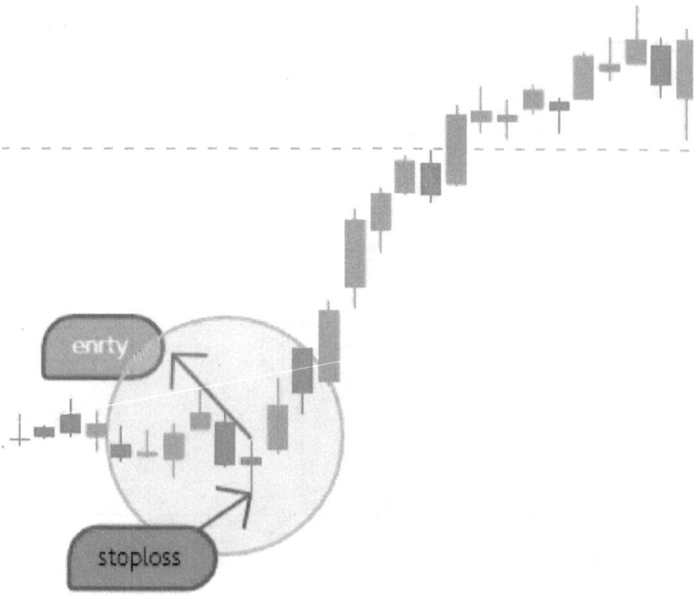

Spinning top in Downtrend

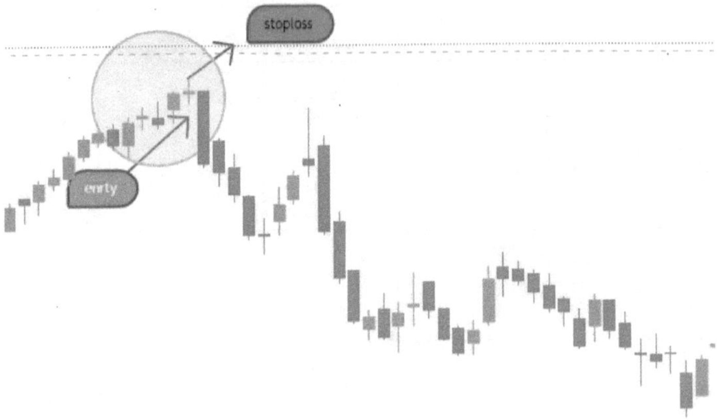

Spinning top in Uptrend

IV

The Dojis

The Dojis have similar implications to the spinning top. What we learned about spinning tops applies to Dojis as well. In fact, the Dojis and spinning tops usually form in a collection, signaling market nervousness.

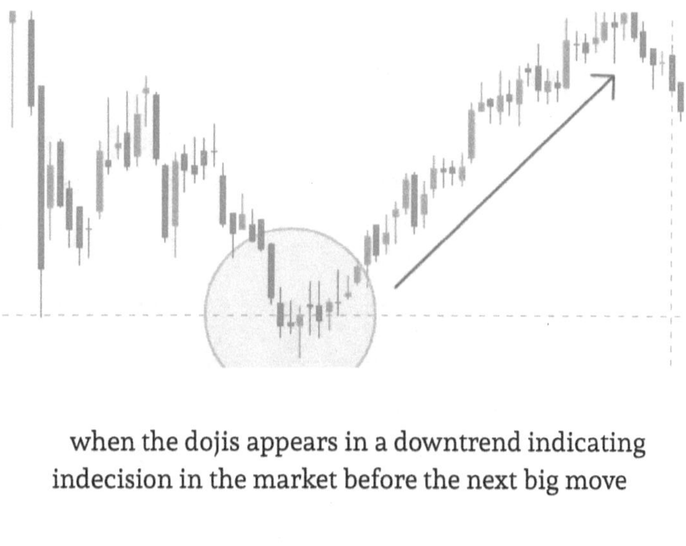

when the dojis appears in a downtrend indicating indecision in the market before the next big move

when the doji appears after a healthy uptrend after which the market reverses its direction and corrects

V

The Hammer

Enter Caption

The bullish hammer is a major candlestick pattern that develops around the bottom of a trend. A hammer consists of a small genuine body at the upper end of the trading range and a large lower shadow. The longer and lower the shadow, the more bullish the pattern.

The Hanging man

A "Hanging Man" when it appears at the peak of a trend. One candlestick and a top reversal pattern combine to form the bearish hanging man. A market peak is indicated by a hanging man. Only when an uptrend comes before the hanging man is it considered a hanging man. The bearish hanging man pattern indicates to sell pressure because it appears after a high.

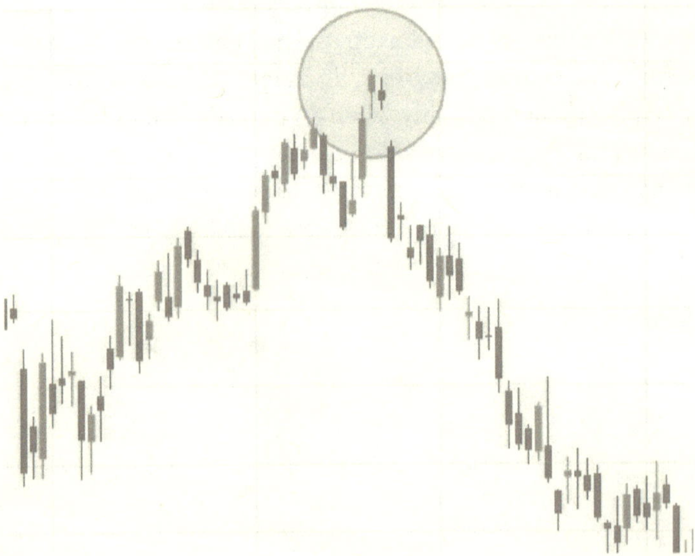

Enter Caption

The shooting star

The final single candlestick pattern we will cover before going on to multiple candlestick patterns is the shooting star. The shooting star is a popular candlestick pattern to trade because of its strong price movement.

The shooting star looks just like an inverted Hammer

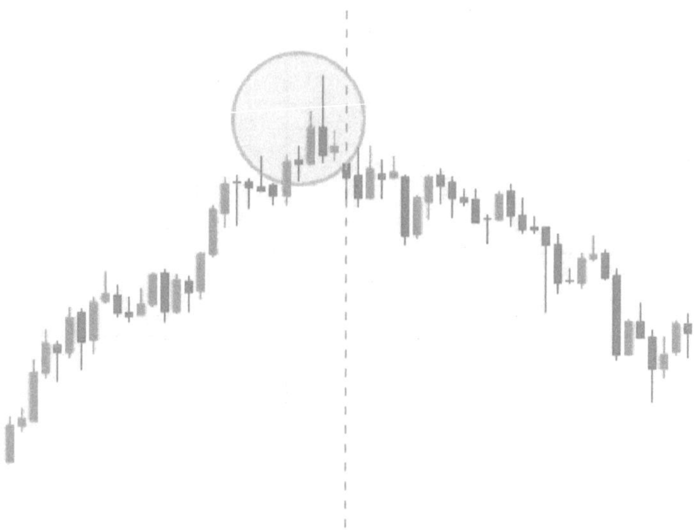

shooting star in uptrend and after that price fall

shooting star in downtrend and after that price rise

VI

The Engulfing Pattern

It takes two trading sessions for the engulfing pattern to develop. A small candle on day 1 and a relatively long candle on day 2, which appears to engulf the day 1 candle, are characteristics of an engulfing pattern. The engulfing pattern is referred to as the "Bullish Engulfing" pattern if it emerges at the bottom of the trend. The engulfing pattern is referred to as the "Bearish Engulfing" pattern if it emerges at the upper end of the trend.

Enter Caption

Bullish Engulfing

At the bottom of the downtrend, a two-candlestick pattern known as the bullish engulfing pattern emerges. This pattern, as its name implies, is bullish, which favors the trader to go long.

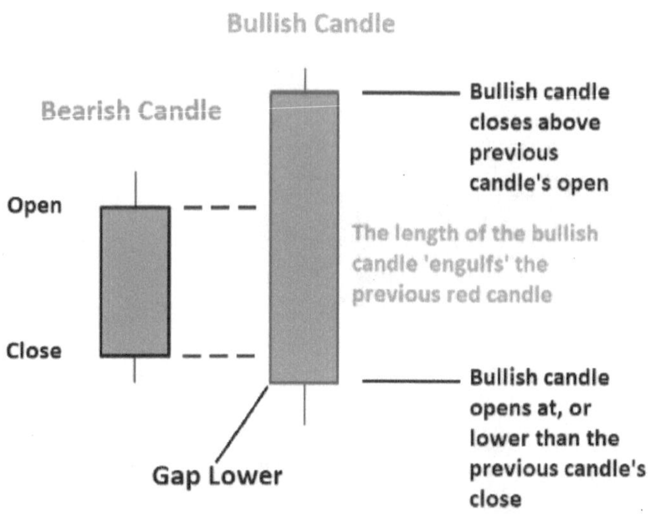

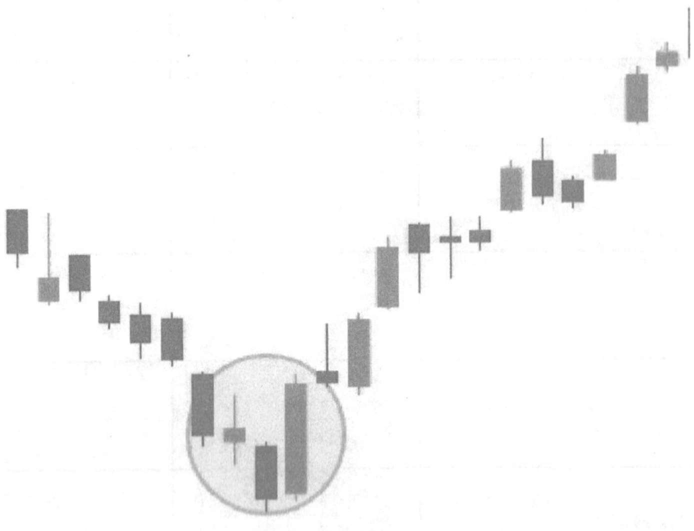

Bullish engulfing

Bearish Engulfing

A two candlestick pattern that arises at the upper end of the trend is known as a bearish engulfing pattern. Though one must approach it from a shorting perspective, the process of thinking about it is still very similar to the bullish engulfing pattern.

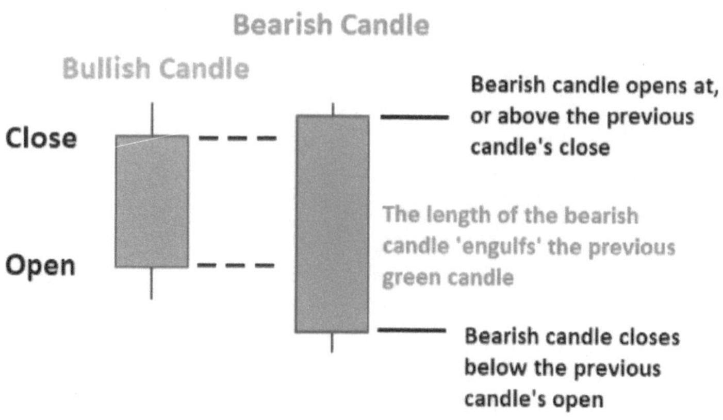

Enter Caption

VII

The Piercing Pattern

A two-day candlestick price pattern known as a piercing pattern indicates the possibility of a short-term trend reversal from an upward to a downward direction. The first day's opening close to the high and closing close to the low with an average or wider trading range are part of the pattern. In addition, there is a gap down after the first day of trading, with the second day opening close to the low and closing close to the high. Additionally, the close ought to be a candlestick that spans at least half of the upward length of the red candlestick body from the day before.

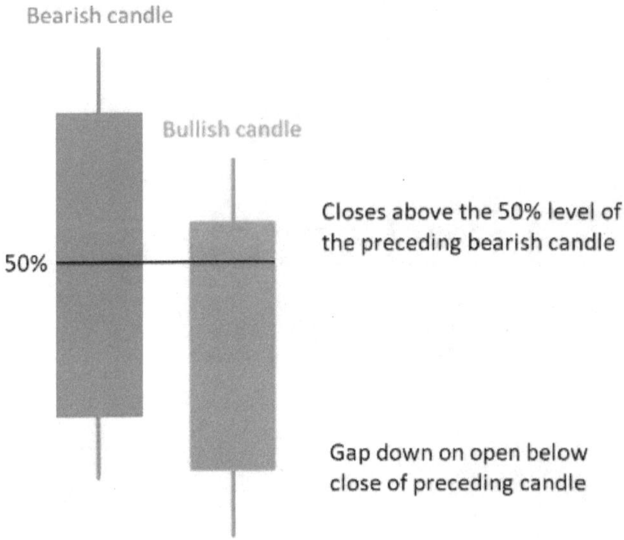

Enter Caption

Enter Caption

VIII

The Dark Cloud Cover

A large black candle forms a dark cloud over the previous candle in the Dark Cloud Cover pattern. The majority of traders believe that the Dark Cloud Cover Pattern is only beneficial when it appears after an uptrend or general rise in price. The pattern becomes more significant as prices rise in indicating a possible move to the downside.

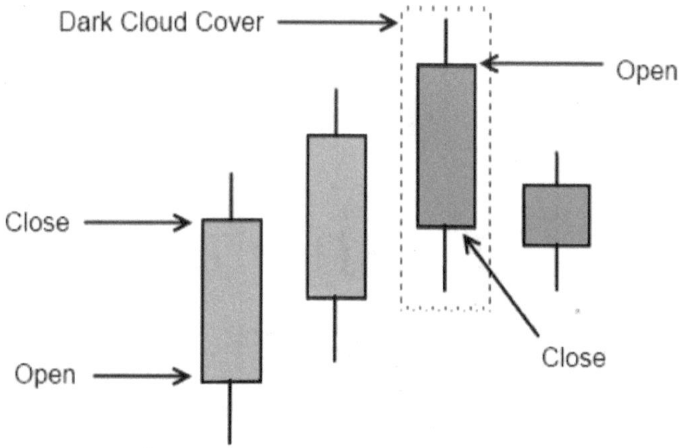

Enter Caption

IX

The Bullish Harami Pattern

At the bottom of the chart is a bullish pattern known as the bullish harami. Like the engulfing pattern, the bullish harami pattern develops over the course of two days.

Enter Caption

X

The Bearish Harami Pattern

Bearish harami typically appears at the end of a bullish rally and suggests a possible downward reversal. When the number of sellers exceeds that of buyers and the buyers become worn out, this pattern emerges.

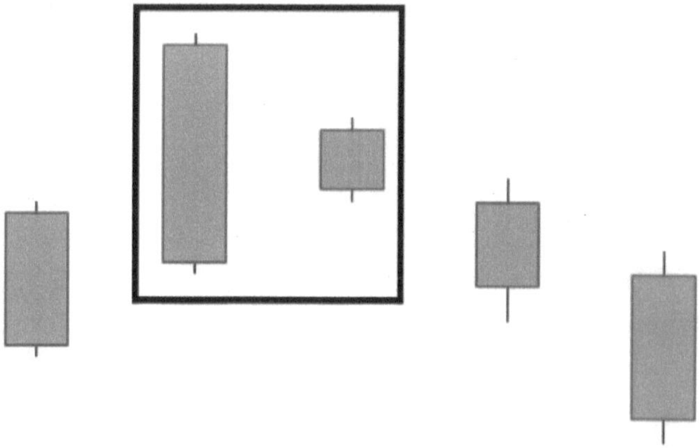

Enter Caption

XI

The Morning star Pattern

A three-day candlestick pattern that is bullish in nature is called the morning star. It is a pattern of downtrend reversal. Three consecutive candlesticks are combined to create the pattern. At the very end of a downward trend, the morning star emerges.

XII

The Evening Star Pattern

Similar to the morning star, the evening star is bearish. The evening star emerges when an uptrend is nearing its peak. The evening star forms with three candles and changes over the course of three trading sessions, just like the morning star.

Enter Caption

XIII

SUPPORT AND RESISTANCE

During a downtrend, prices fall due to excess supply versus demand. Those holding off on purchasing shares find the prices to be more attractive as they decline. Demand that would have been gradually rising will eventually reach a point where supply and demand are equal. Prices will then cease to decline. This is support.

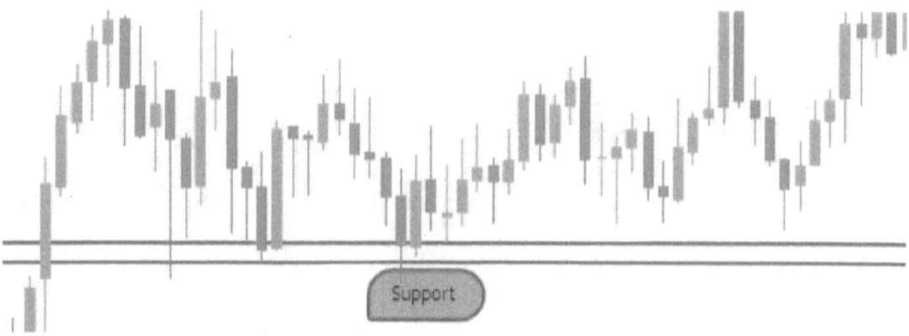

The reverse of support is resistance. The reason for price increases is a surplus of demand over supply. There will come a time when the desire to sell will surpass the desire to buy as prices rise.

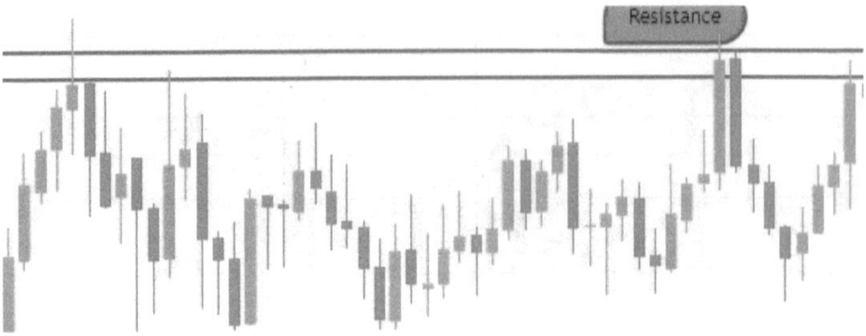

Enter Caption

XIV

Double Bottom

A double bottom pattern is a traditional technical analysis charting formation that denotes a significant shift in trend and a reversal of momentum from an earlier decline in market trading. A security or index may experience a decline, a rebound, another decline to the same or a comparable level, and then another rebound (which could lead to a new uptrend). It appears that the double bottom is a "W." The low that has been touched twice is now regarded as a crucial support level. The upside has new potential as long as those two lows hold.

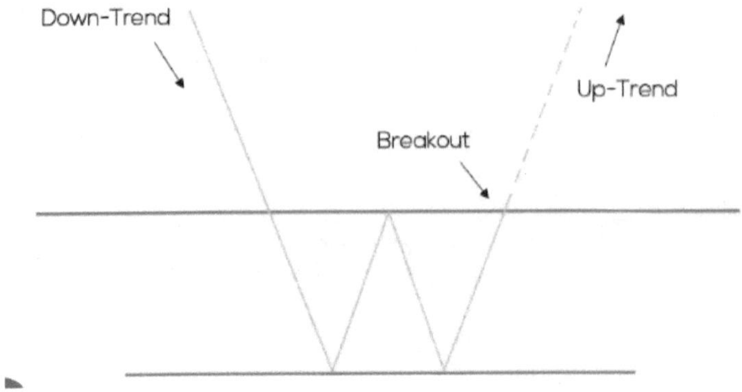

Enter Caption

Enter Caption

XV
Double Top

When an asset hits a high price two times in a row with a moderate decline in between, a double top is a very bearish technical reversal pattern. Once the asset's price drops below a level of support equivalent to the low between the two previous highs, it is confirmed.

Enter Caption

XVI

Head and Shoulder

Technical analysis uses a head and shoulders pattern. A particular type of chart pattern indicates a trend reversal from bullish to bearish. The pattern shows up as a baseline with three peaks, the middle peak being the highest and the outer two being close in height.

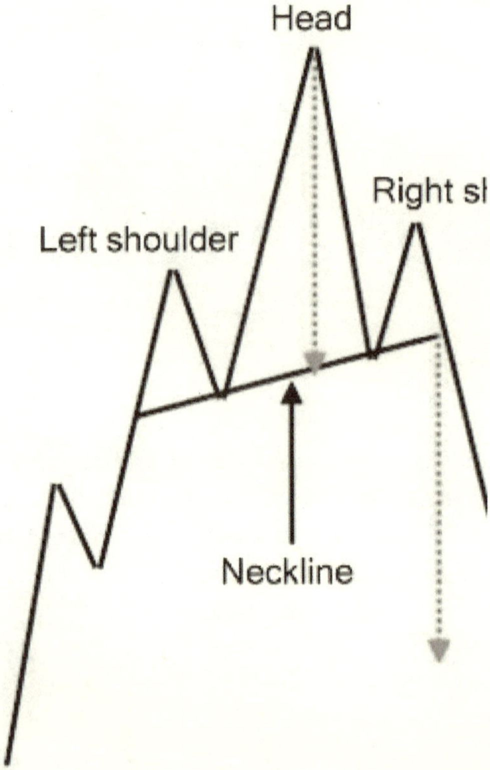

Enter Caption

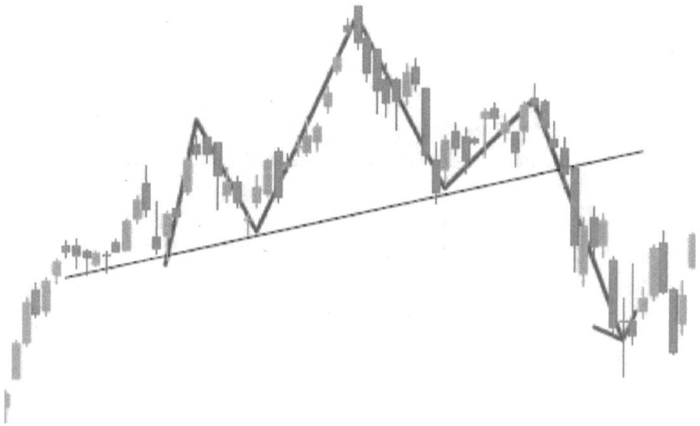

Enter Caption

XVII

Inverse Head and Shoulders

A bullish chart formation that may indicate a downtrend reversal is the inverse head and shoulders pattern. It is not to be confused with the bearish head and shoulders chart pattern.

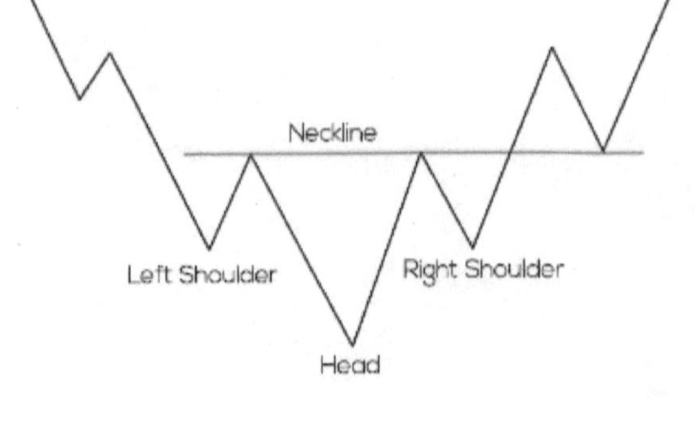

Enter Caption

XVIII

Cup and Handle Pattern

A cup and handle is regarded as a bullish signal, and lower trading volume is usually seen on the right side of the pattern. It could take seven weeks or 65 weeks for the pattern to form.

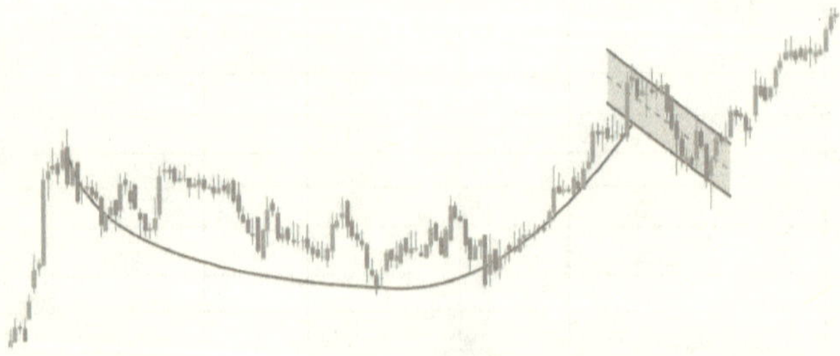

Enter Caption

XIX
Ascending Triangle

Technical analysis uses an ascending triangle as a chart pattern. It is produced by price movements that make it possible to draw a rising trendline along the swing lows and a horizontal line along the swing highs. Triangle is formed by the two lines.

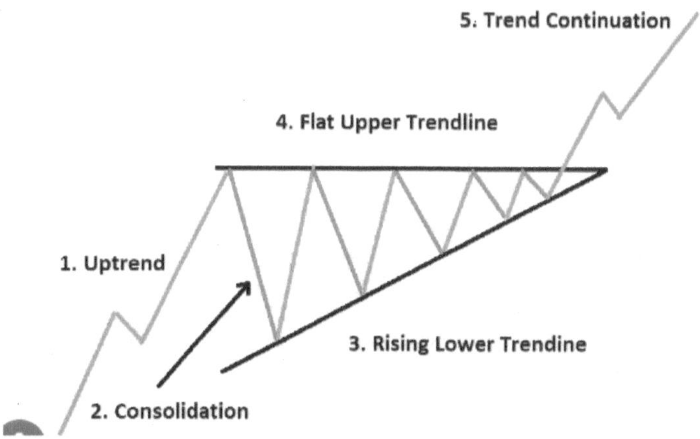

Enter Caption

Enter Caption

XX

Symmetrical triangle

Triangles that are symmetrical indicate a break in the current trend as bulls and bears find balance. But once the price breaks out of the triangle decisively, it usually indicates the beginning of a new trend or the continuation of the previous trend.

Breakout on upper side lead to uptrend and vie versa

XXI
Rounding bottom

It can be recognized by a sequence of price changes that visually represent a "U". Rounding bottoms are the the end of lengthy declining trends and indicate a change in the direction of long-term price movement.

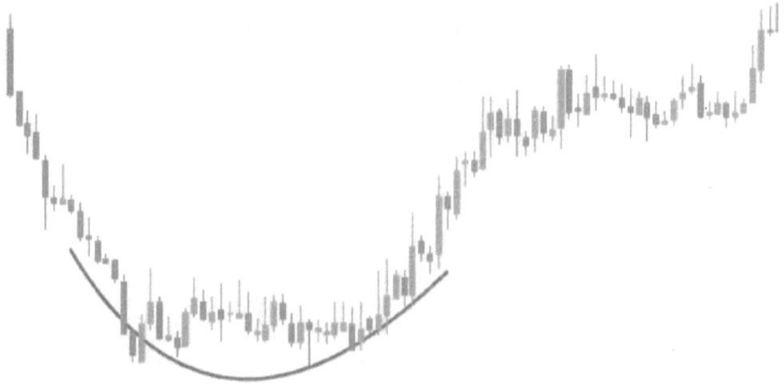

Enter Caption

XXII

Pannants or Flags

A pennant is a kind of continuation pattern in technical analysis. It forms as a result of a significant movement inside a security area called the flagpole. The second half of the flagpole is represented by the breakout movement that occurs in the same direction as the first large movement, after which there is a consolidation period with converging trend lines (the pennant).

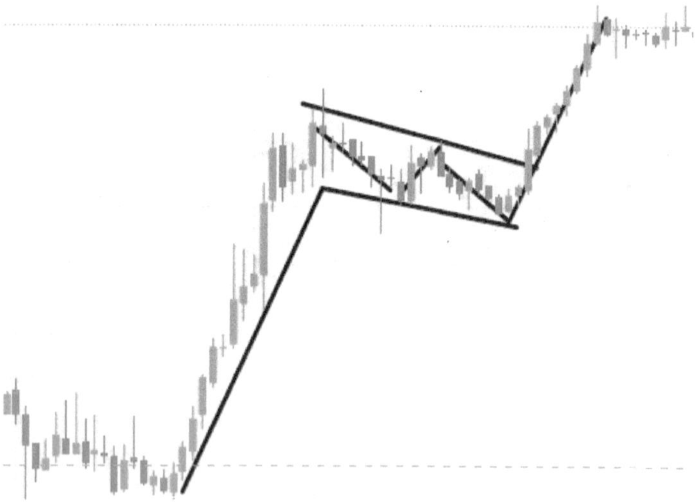

Bullish pennant or flag

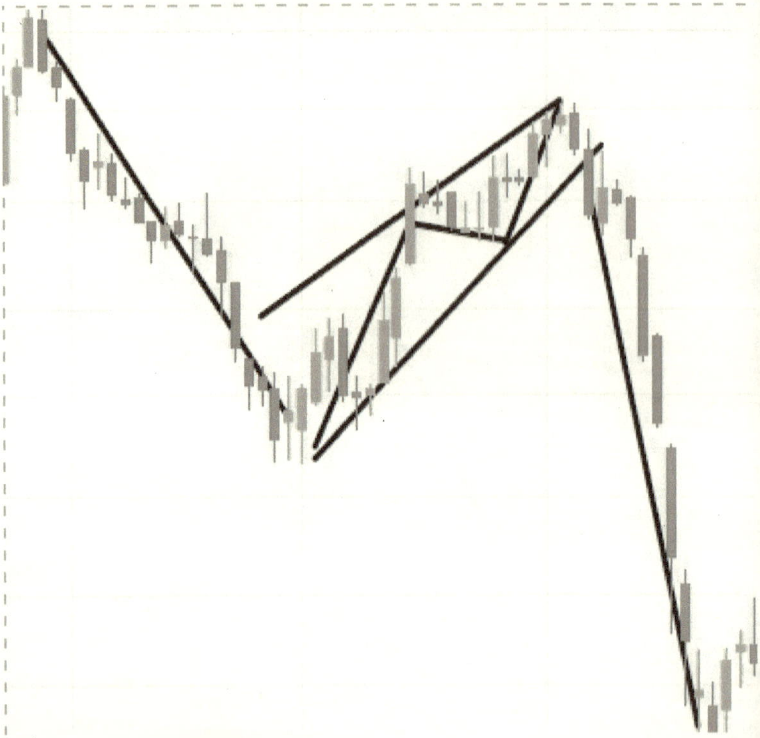

Bearish pennants or flag

Finally

but just as importantly, if in doubt, avoid it.

www.ingramcontent.com/pod-product-compliance
Lightning Source LLC
LaVergne TN
LVHW090431210926
848480LV00002B/777
9798894155883